AF470292

HELL

A DESIGNATED PLACE

Dennis D. Helton

Copyright © 2023 by Dennis Helton
All Rights Reserved
Printed in the United States of America
Dennis Helton
200 Home Place Drive
Easley, SC 29640

ISBN 979-8-9873593-6-5

All Scripture quotes are from the King James Bible

No part of this work may be reproduced without the expressed consent of the publisher, except for brief quotes, whether by electronic, photocopying, recording, or information storage and retrieval systems.

Address All Inquiries To:
THE OLD PATHS PUBLICATIONS, Inc.
142 Gold Flume Way
Cleveland, Georgia, U.S.A.

Web: www.theoldpathspublications.com
E-mail: TOP@theoldpathspublications.com

DEDICATION

This work is dedicated to my faithful wife, Christine, of 60 years.

Dennis D. Helton
January 2023

TABLE OF CONTENTS

CHAPTER 1
HELL – AN EVERLASTING FIRE
A Literal Place

> *"Then shall he say also unto them on the left hand, Depart from me, ye cursed, into* ***everlasting fire****, prepared for the devil and his angels."* **Matthew 25:41**

Getting right to the point, Hell is a literal place where lost people go upon death.

The damnation of Hell is the fire of God's anger fastening upon a sinner. Jesus had more to say about Hell than any other speaker or writer in the Bible. How can it be that Jesus Christ, who taught so authoritatively the importance of love and forgiveness, could speak such words as these? Since He is the **Creator** (Colossians 1:16), the coming **Judge** (John 5:22), and the only man who has died and risen eternally or permanently from the dead (2 Corinthians 5:14-15), we would do well to believe and heed his warnings. Jesus knows whereof He speaks.

Deniers Of Hell-Fire:

At the outset, let the reader beware that there are well known and respected national preachers that question a Hell that has fire and some even deny that there is a literal place called Hell. Some of these religionists will be named later in this writing.

(NOTE: For some time, this writer has observed the shallowness and lack of spiritual discernment of many well-known "so-called" preachers.)

CHAPTER 2

WHERE DO THE DEAD GO?

Only Two Places

The Bible teaches that there are only two places that the dead go to upon death, **Heaven or Hell**.

Heaven

Heaven is a place of light, holiness, bliss, and glory.

> **Revelation 21:4** *"And God shall wipe away all tears from their eyes; and there shall be no more death, neither sorrow, nor crying, neither shall there be any more pain: for the former things are passed away."*

> **Isaiah 11:6-9** *"The wolf also shall dwell with the lamb, and the leopard shall lie down with the kid; and the calf and the young lion and the fatling together; and a little*
> *child shall lead them.* **7** *And the*
> *cow and the bear shall feed; their young ones shall lie down together: and the lion shall eat*
> *straw like the ox.* **8** *And the*
> *sucking child shall play on the hole*

of the asp, and the weaned child shall put his hand on the cockatrice' den. ***9*** *They shall not hurt nor destroy in all my holy mountain: for the earth shall be full of the knowledge of the LORD, as the waters cover the sea."*

Hell

Hell is a place of darkness, pain, agony, and horror.

Mark 9:47-48 *"... to be cast into hell fire:* ***48*** *Where their worm dieth not, and the fire is not quenched."*

The saved go to Heaven and the unsaved go to Hell. Both are designated permanent abodes (Hell is cast into **the lake of fire** – **Revelation 20:13-14**).

"And the sea gave up the dead which were in it; and death and hell delivered up the dead which were in them: and they were judged every man according to their works. ***14 And death and hell were cast into the lake of fire.*** *This is the second death."*

There is probably no other doctrine deplored and denied more than the teaching of a literal Hell.

Death is the end of all **joy** for the *lost*. Death is the end of all **grief** for the *saved*. Only the individuals themselves, and they alone, can make the choice of their eternal dwelling place.

Of course, there are false teachings concerning life after death. Some teach that there is a middle-ground (limbo state; neutral zone) between Heaven and Hell such as a "so called" **purgatory** while many others teach various forms of **reincarnation**. The Bible does not teach either of these.

Purgatory

Purgatory is a man-made fabricated intermediate place of cleansing or purging of sin.)

Reincarnation

Reincarnation is a false philosophy of paganism that teaches that we pay for [atone] our own sins by self-improvement through **many** lives, based on karmic law. Karmic law says that if we do evil in this life, we pay for it in the next life. However, we can slowly perfect ourselves through multiple lives and eventually **everyone** will reach the goal of perfection, salvation, or liberation.)

Christ is the Judge and the final high court. Jesus plainly stated that unbelievers were of their father, the devil. Neither are the devil's children spiritual brethren to God's children. There is no appeal after death.

CHAPTER 3

ARE ALL PEOPLE THE CHILDREN OF GOD?

The Fatherhood of God and the brotherhood of man is not an accurate description. We are all children of God only in the sense of creation or the natural birth. The unsaved are not children of God in the sense of the new creation until they become born again. **2 Peter 1:4:**

> *"Whereby are given unto us exceeding great and precious promises: that by these ye might be partakers of the divine nature, having escaped the corruption that is in the world through lust."*

We become children of God by re-creation (2 Corinthians 5:17) called the new birth (spiritual birth) that Jesus said was absolutely imperative. (**John** 3:3, 5, 7; 2 **Corinthians** 5:17**; Titus** 3:5).

> **2 Corinthians 5:17** *"Therefore if any man be in Christ, he is a new creature: old things are passed away; behold, all things are become new."*

> **John 3:3** *"Jesus answered and said unto him, Verily, verily, I say unto thee, Except a man be born*

> *again, he cannot see the kingdom of God."* **John 3:5** *"Jesus answered, Verily, verily, I say unto thee, Except a man be born of water and of the Spirit, he cannot enter into the kingdom of God."* **John 3:7** *"Marvel not that I said unto thee, Ye must be born again."*

> **Titus 3:5** *"Not by works of righteousness which we have done, but according to his mercy he saved us, by the washing of regeneration, and renewing of the Holy Ghost;"*

It is very significant that Jesus spoke the words of the necessity of being "born again" to a highly religious but unsaved man (Nicodemus of **John** 3:3-7). The unsaved are brethren only in the sense that we all are physical descendants of Adam and Eve and are all of one blood **Acts 17:26:**

> **Acts 17:26** *"And hath made of one blood all nations of men for to dwell on all the face of the earth, and hath determined the times before appointed, and the bounds of their habitation;"*

Unbelievers

Jesus plainly stated that unbelievers were of their father, the devil. Neither are the devil's children spiritual brethren to God's children. **John 8:44:**

> *"Ye are of your father the devil, and the lusts of your father ye will do. He was a murderer from the beginning, and abode not in the truth, because there is no truth in him. When he speaketh a lie, he speaketh of his own: for he is a liar, and the father of it."*

Perhaps the unsaved person may say, "I haven't made up my mind yet." If a sinner has heard the truth of the Gospel of Jesus Christ only once and has not accepted God's provision for his guilt of sin, he has made a choice already (simply by rejecting Jesus Christ). The Bible says that a person that has not believed in Jesus is condemned already. **John 3:18**:

> *"...but he that believeth not is **condemned already**, because he hath not believed in the name of the only begotten Son of God"*

God often delays the punishment of sin for a while, but it is laid up in store till the measure be full and the day of divine patience is over. **Job 21:28-30:**

> ***28*** *"For ye say, Where is the house of the prince? and where are the dwelling places of the wicked?* ***29*** *Have ye not asked them that go by the way? and do ye not know their tokens,* ***30*** *That the wicked is reserved to the day of destruction? they shall be brought forth to the day of wrath."*

Ecclesiastes 8:11

> *"Because sentence against an evil work is not executed speedily, therefore the heart of the sons of men is fully set in them to do evil."*

Is Salvation a Gradual Process?

Salvation is instantaneous (not progressive). By hearing the Word of God and being drawn and convicted of sin by the Holy Spirit, a sinner acting in repentance and by faith is supernaturally birthed into God's family in a moment of time. A sinner has innumerable opportunities to be saved: 365 days each year; 16 waking-hours each day; 60 minutes each hour; etc. It only takes a moment in time to be born again by the Spirit of God. There will be no second-chances nor excuses for the lost sinner before the Great White Throne judgment bar of God (Revelation 20:11).

Instantaneous New Birth

The new birth or being "born again" is not a gradual process but is a very brief supernatural act of God. **1 Peter 3:18:**

> *"For Christ also hath once suffered for sins, the just for the unjust, that he might bring us to God, being put to death in the flesh, but quickened by the Spirit:"*

The new-born child of God does have need of gradually growing "in" grace but not a need of growing "into" grace> **I Peter 2:2**:

> *"As newborn babes, desire the sincere milk of the word, that ye may grow thereby:"*

One website stated it like this:

> "Do we "doubt" our Salvation? HE has set Eternity in our hearts (Ecclesiastes 3:11). We want to believe but we doubt we know how. You have instilled in your heart a passion for more? Do you want an understanding of something beyond your mind? It is a special unsatisfiable part of you that needs understanding beyond this world, it is SPIRITUAL understanding. Do you find yourself "hating" sin (this is good, you are beginning to hate the things GOD hates)? Do you search for WHO JESUS IS and why HE died for our sins? Have you prayed (no matter how feeble it may seem) to know GOD? Have

you repented your sins and begin to read about GOD'S promises (no matter how uncompromisable they may seem) and been encouraged just a little as you find they are True? Is your desire for Truth beyond anything else within your inner most Being? Are you beginning to know that JESUS not only lived on this earth but because of all of the Prophecies verifying (some written 600 years before it happened) HIS dying for our sins you are beginning to KNOW this is True? Are you beginning to Trust something greater than yourself and discovering this is GOD? Are you absolutely astounded that JESUS was raised from the dead (as verified by more than 500 witnesses, to help you in your unbelief) which confirms GOD'S Scriptures? Have you ever done something you did not really want to do (Faith begins) and later found out it brought JOY beyond this world? Have you prayed this prayer, Psalm 119:169, "Let my cry come near before THEE, O'LORD: give me understanding according to THY WORD..." Have you found you are more discerning of right and wrong? The SPIRIT is in you and you want not only to follow JESUS but you want to be like HIM! Did you repent and ask GOD to forgive you and know you are forgiven, did you tell HIM you know JESUS is HIS SON, did you tell HIM you know JESUS rose from the dead? Then there is no reason to doubt because salvation is immediate, understanding is gradual. (Salvation is Immediate, Understanding is Gradual! - PURPOSE FOR YOU, accessed, 1/13/23)

If a person refuses to believe on the Son for everlasting life, he is presently under the wrath of God and death will culminate the punishment. **John 3:36:**

> *"He that believeth on the Son hath everlasting life: and he that believeth not the Son shall not see life; but the wrath of God abideth on him."*

An unsaved person is presently under the wrath of God and eternal judgment is imminent (may occur any moment). While there is life, there is hope, but there is great danger and little hope for those who continue to neglect ((procrastinate) salvation. **Hebrews 2:3:**

> *"How shall we escape, if we neglect so great salvation; which at the first began to be spoken by the Lord, and was confirmed unto us by them that heard Him."*

CHAPTER 4
WHAT DID JESUS SAY ABOUT HELL?

Jesus preached on Hell about fifty-six times in the four Gospels and preached on Heaven only twenty-four times. In the Book of Matthew, Jesus preached on Hell in His first sermon (*Sermon on the Mount*). In the last sermon of His ministry (*Olivet Discourse*), Jesus preached on Hell. Jesus preached more on Hell than Paul did. Jesus was a hell-fire and brimstone Preacher. Of the twelve times that Hell (Gehenna) is expressly stated in the New Testament, eleven of them were spoken by Jesus Himself (by James once).

The warnings of Jesus in Mark 9 speak an ominous and eternal wrath to those who would lightly regard hell-fire. **Mark 9:43-44:**

> *"And if thy hand offend thee, cut it off: it is better for thee to enter into life maimed, than having two hands to go into H**ell, into the fire** that never shall be quenched: Where their worm dieth not, and **the fire is not quenched**."*

Mark 9:45-46:

> *"And if thy foot offend thee, cut if off: it is better for thee to enter halt into life, than having two feet to be*

*cast int Hell, **into the fire** that never shall be quenched: Where their worm dieth not, and **the fire not quenched**."*

Mark 9:47-48:

*"And if thine eye offend thee, pluck it out: it is better for thee to enter into the kingdom of God with one eye, than having two eyes to be cast into Hell **fire**: Where their worm dieth not, and **the fire is not quenched**."*

D. L. Moody said,

"Some come to me and say, 'You do not really believe there is such a thing as everlasting retribution and future punishment, do you?'

Yes, I do! The same Christ who talked to us about that bright upper world has given us a picture of the lost. In **Luke 16:29-31**, it has been drawn very vividly by the Master Himself. We hear a voice coming up out of the lost world—of the man that was once upon the earth and fared sumptuously every day, yet was lost, not for time but for eternity.

Over and over again, Christ warned those who hung upon His words. Once, in speaking to His disciples, He spoke about the worm that dieth not; about one being "cast into Hell...where their **worm** dieth not."

Luke 16:29-31:

> *"Abraham saith unto him, They have Moses and the prophets; let them hear them.* ***30*** *And he said, Nay, father Abraham: but if one went unto them from the dead, they will repent.* ***31*** *And he said unto him, If they hear not Moses and the prophets, neither will they be persuaded, though one rose from the dead."*

The unbeliever need not worry about the meaning of "their worm" and what kind of fire is in Hell. The sinner needs to run to God for mercy before it is too late; there is no such thing as a "second chance." Most everyone has had thousands of chances before they died. In one month alone, a sinner has available: 30 days times 16 waking hours per day times 60 minutes in the hour which translates to: 30 X 16 X 60 = 28,800 minutes. Again, it doesn't take a full minute to repent and believe unto salvation for salvation itself is instantaneous and only requires a very brief moment of time.

Sin will reap sorrow and if not repented of...will reap everlasting sorrow. **Psalm 32:10:**

> *"Many sorrows shall be to the wicked: but he that trusteth in the LORD, mercy shall compass him about."*

CHAPTER 5

IS HELL A LITERAL PLACE?

Hell is not just separation from God or a state of mind. Hell is a literal place just as Heaven is a literal place. You can't believe in a literal Heaven unless you believe in a literal Hell. If Hell is symbolic or figurative, so then is Heaven. The same Bible declares both to be literal places.

The question has to arise, "If Hell is a literal place of eternal punishment, why do I never hear a warning of it from the pulpit?" For one thing, most preachers do not have the backbone (spiritual intestinal fortitude) to declare it. Many preachers mean well, but they are influenced greatly about numbers in the pews and security in their retirement. They know that they will lose church members if they preach too strongly about Hell and some would probably be dismissed from their denominational membership.

Of course, many liberal preachers don't even believe in a literal Hell. Some well-known pastors and evangelists are uncertain as to the state of Hell and relegate it to mere isolation from God (and it is "isolation"). But Hell is much more than separation from God. It is torment; it is anguish of soul; it is great suffering. **Luke 16:23-24:**

> *23 "And in hell he lift up his eyes, being in torments, and seeth Abraham afar off, and Lazarus in his bosom.* **24** *And he cried and*

> *said, Father Abraham, have mercy on me, and send Lazarus, that he may dip the tip of his finger in water, and cool my tongue; for I am tormented in this flame."*

One of America's best-known evangelists says that he does not preach that there is fire in Hell because he is not sure. Many "so-called" preachers are only drawing their breath and a salary. Preachers should be warning men of the consequences of sin and Hell (if they believe it themselves).

One professing atheist has indited many Christians of our complacent attitude toward Hell by stating that if he really believed in Hell as an awful place of eternal torment as Christians claim to believe, he would crawl through miles of broken glass in order to warn others to flee God's wrath. That sounds like a very good sermon from an unbeliever to a believer...something to seriously consider!

AARP Poll

The AARP Magazine polled its members (age 50 and over) about their belief in life after death.

- Ninety-four percent (94%) responded that they believed in God.
- Eighty-six percent (86%) said they believed in Heaven.
- Only seventy percent (70%) believed in Hell.

As any true Bible believer can see, there is a discrepancy here. You can't believe differently about the existence of Heaven and Hell. You can't have one without the other. The only true source of the reality of Heaven and Hell is from God's Word, the Bible. Unlearned, untaught, and unsaved people believe that which appeals to them (such as a everlasting utopian Heaven for all). A horrible place of eternal torment has no appeal to anyone (especially to the carnal mind). Death to the wicked is the King of Terror.

D. L. Moody said,

> "Death and judgment were a constant source of fear to me till I realized that neither shall ever have any hold on a child of God."

Death to the saints is the end of terrors and the commencement of glory.

C. H. Spurgeon said,

> "There is an essential difference between the decease of the godly and the death of the ungodly. Death comes to the ungodly man as a penal infliction, but to the righteous as a summons to his Father's palace. To the sinner it is an execution; to the saint, an undressing from his sins and infirmities."

There are only two roads to eternal future. Heaven and Hell are eternal realities.

The Secular World & Apostates & Hell

What the secular world, some evangelists, preachers, and theologians have to say about Hell?

In these last days near the "End of the Age," it has become commonplace for theologians to question the biblical doctrine of Hell. Even among "professing" Christians, there is a deep-seeded doubt as to the eternal punishment of the lost. Most of the time, it is unspoken or whispered quietly. The writer thinks that liberal preachers may be afraid that a literal Hell may be disproved so he does not preach it.

The skeptics usually pose the same "time-worn" questions concerning a literal Hell:

1. The reality of Hell itself as a place
2. The length of Hell's punishment
3. The soul's eternal non-existence (annihilation)
4. A loving God would not be so cruel as to punish one in such a manner?
5. The fire of Hell is symbolic
6. Hell is the inner suffering that one makes for himself
7. Hell is the sufferings here upon earth
    a. ...and the list goes on and on.

What Has Happened in Modern Pulpits?

What has happened to Hell and its punishment in modern pulpits?

(The following information copied from *Fundamental Baptist Information Service* and Distributed by Way of Life Literature, P.O. Box 610368, Port Huron, MI 48061. 866-295-4143, fbns@wayoflife.org)

- In 1986, **Martin Marty**, senior editor of the Christian Century, spoke of the "passing of Hell from modern consciousness" as "one of the major if still largely undocumented modern trends" - (Marty, "Whatever Happened to Hell, The Lutheran , April 2, 1986).

- In 1986, *Today* editor **Kenneth Kantzer** said that he had not heard a sermon on Hell in 30 years.
- In its June 10, 2002, edition, the *Los Angeles Times* published an article entitled "Hold the Fire and Brimstone," documenting the fact that "mention of Hell from pulpits is at an all-time low." **Bill Faris**, pastor of Crown Valley Vineyard Christian Fellowship, told the Times that though he believes in Hell he doesn't preach on it because, "It isn't sexy enough." The Times observed that not only does Faris not preach on Hell but, "his flock shows little interest in it."
- **Harvey Cox Jr**., a liberal religious historian and professor at Harvard Divinity School, said, "You can go to a whole lot of churches week after week, and you'd be startled even to hear a mention of Hell."
- **Bruce Shelly**, professor of church history at *Denver Theological Seminary*, observed that Hell is "just too negative" and that "churches today feel the need to be appealing rather than demanding."
- The *Los Angeles Times* did a search of **Rick Warren's** Saddleback Church's web site and discovered that though there are hundreds of sermons for sale on all sorts of topics, there is not even one on Hell.
- The denial of Hell came from the lips of **Pope John Paul II.** He stated that Hell is not a physical place but "the state of those who freely and definitely separate themselves from God." He denied that Hell is a place of fiery torment and described if rather as "the pain, frustration and

emptiness of life without God." He further claimed that Hell is not a punishment imposed externally by God and that eternal damnation "is not God's work but is actually our own doing" (Reuters, July 29, 1999).

The Pope's Anemic Doctrine

The Bible sheds a lot of light upon the pope's anemic doctrine: Mark 9:44, 46, 48; Matthew 5:22; 18:9; Matthew 18:8; 25:41; Luke 3:17; Luke 16:24; Matthew 13:42, 50; Jude 7; Revelation 14:10; 20:10; 21:8.

- **Billy Graham**:

  "I think that Hell essentially is separation from God forever. And that is the worst Hell that I can think of. But I think people have a hard time believing God is going to allow people to burn in literal fire forever. I think the fire that is mentioned in the Bible is a burning thirst for God that can never be quenched" (Graham, *Orlando Sentinel*, Orlando, Florida, April 10, 1983.

  "The only thing I could say for sure is that Hell means separation from God. We are separated from His light, from His fellowship. That is going to be Hell. **When it comes to a literal fire, I don't preach it because I'm not sure about it.** When the Scripture uses fire concerning Hell, that is possibly an illustration of how terrible it's going to be—not fire but something worse, a thirst for God that cannot be quenched" (Billy Graham, interview with Richard Ostling, *Time magazine*, Nov. 15, 1993).

If the revered Billy Graham has the audacity to make such an atrocious statement concerning literal fire in Hell, then this writer has the audacity to quote him. Some Christians are swooned or religiously hypnotized by big-named personalities and would not dare question them for fear of reprisal. Perhaps they are even ignorant on doctrine themselves. The Bible sheds a lot of light on the subject of Hell-fire if the reader prefers to heed the Words of Jesus against unenlightened preachers. **Mark 9:43-48**:

> ***43*** *"And if thy hand offend thee,*
> *cut it off: it is better for thee to*
> *enter into life maimed, than having*
> *two hands to go into hell, into the*
> *fire that never shall be quenched:*
> ***44*** *Where their worm dieth not,*
> *and the fire is not quenched.* ***45***
> *And if thy foot offend thee, cut it*
> *off: it is better for thee to enter halt*
> *into life, than having two feet to be*
> *cast into hell, into the fire that*
> *never shall be quenched:* ***46***
> *Where their worm dieth not, and*
> *the fire is not quenched.* ***47*** *And if*
> *thine eye offend thee, pluck it out:*
> *it is better for thee to enter into the*
> *kingdom of God with one eye,*
> *than having two eyes to be cast*
> *into hell fire:* ***48*** *Where their worm*
> *dieth not, and the fire is not*
> *quenched."*

➢ **Robert Schuller**:

"And what is 'hell'? It is the loss of pride that naturally follows separation from God—the ultimate and unfailing source of our soul's sense of self-respect. 'My God, my God, why hast thou forsaken me?' was Christ's encounter with Hell. In that 'hellish' death our Lord experienced the ultimate horror-humiliation, shame, and loss of pride as a human being. A PERSON IS IN HELL WHEN HE HAS LOST HIS SELF-ESTEEM. Can you imagine any condition more tragic than to live life and eternity in shame?" - (Schuller, *Self-Esteem: The New Reformation*, 1982, pp. 14-15, 93).

➢ **CHRISTIANITIY TODAY**; Two years after Schuller published Self-Esteem: The New Reformation, the editors of Christianity Today examined his theology and, amazingly, concluded that he is not a heretic. Consider an excerpt form an August 10, 1984, Christianity Today article by **Kenneth Kantzer** and **Paul Fromer**: "He believes all the 'fundamental' doctrines of traditional fundamentalism. He adheres to every line of the Apostles' Creed with a tenacity born of deep conviction. ...he avowed belief in a literal Hell. He was not sure about its location, and THE FIRE IS TO BE UNDERSTOOD FIGURATIVELY..."

➢ **GORDON-CONWELL THEOLOGICAL SEMINARY:**

"Some students and professors at Gordon Conwell Theological Seminary question and even deny the historic Christian and biblical doctrine of eternal punishment...seminarian **Ed Tayler** argued in the breakfast **discussion that there is no eternal**

torment, although Ed said he believed in Heaven and Hell.

- **Clark Pinnock**:

"Pinnock has enthusiastically praised Edward Fudge's The Fire That Consumes, a book which denies the scriptural doctrine of everlasting damnation and eternal Hell (Christian News Encyclopedia, p. 1702). The book was published by Verdict and praised by such leading evangelicals as F.F. Bruce and also Seventh Day Adventists. Pinnock writes in the March 20, 1987 Christianity Today: 'The fire of Hell does not torment, but rather consumes the wicked' (Christian News, March 23, 1987). **"Let me say at the outset that I consider the concept of Hell as endless torment in body and mind an outrageous doctrine...**How can Christians possible project a deity of such cruelty and vindictiveness whose ways include inflicting everlasting torture upon His creatures, however sinful they may have been? Surely, a God who would do such a thing is more nearly like Satan than like God" (Clark Pinnock, *Criswell Theological Review*, April 2, 1990).

- **Neil Punt**:

"Neil Punt promotes what he calls 'biblical universalism' in the March 20 Christianity Today. He says that 'Biblical universalism does not deny the scriptural teaching concerning the sin of Adam. He argues that many verses in the Bible speak of salvation in terms of all persons. The Bible teaches that

Jesus Christ died for all men but it also says that all those who die without believing in Christ as their only Savior from sin are lost in eternal Hell. In 1980 Eerdmans released Punt's Unconditional Good News: Toward an Understanding of Biblical Universalism in which the author **encouraged ministers not to warn sinners about the dangers of eternal damnation"** (*The Christian News,* March 23, 1987).

➢ **Fuller Theological Seminary**: Fuller Theological Seminary's new doctrinal statement departs from its original position on eternal punishment, simply saying that the wicked shall be separated from God's presence (*F.E.A. News & Views,* Fundamental Evangelistic Association, May/June, 1971).

➢ **Herbert Vander Lugt**, Radio Bible Class:

"A Hell in which all burn in a literal fire does not allow for significant degrees of punishment. It's important to remember that the Bible often uses fire as a symbol" (Herbert Vander Lugt, *What Does the Bible Say about Hell?*, 1990).

➢ **Michael Van Horn** (Former professor Grand Rapids Baptist College and Seminary, GARBC: Before a room full of twenty-two Michigan pastors, Professor Van Horn **denied that there was a literal Heaven or a literal Hell**. He especially denied that there was any 'literal fire' in hell (D.A. Waite, *Four Reasons for Defending the King James Bible, Bible for Today*, 1993, pp. 20, 21).

➢ **Kenneth Kantzer** (Trinity Evangelical Divinity School, former editor, Christianity Today**):**

"But when Jesus spoke of flames, these are most likely figurative warnings" (*U.S. News & World Report*, March 25, 1991).

- **John R.W. Stott**:

"At the recent Evangelical Affirmations conference (sponsored by the National Association of Evangelicals) at Trinity Evangelical Divinity School, co-chaired by Carl F.H. Henry and Kenneth Kantzer, John Stott revealed that he was a proponent of conditional immortality, or annihilationism**, a view that denies eternal punishment in Hell for the unsaved"** (*Calvary Contender*, August 1, 1989).

- **J. I. Packer**:

"*Christianity Today* senior editor J. I. Packer say he does not believe that the essence of Hell is grotesque bodily discomfort. That idea, he conceives, misses the deeper point of the lurid word pictures drawn by Dante and Jesus, and the New Testament writers. He says: **"The essence of Hell is surely an inner misery of helpless remorse,** with recognition that in assigning one to an eternity of self absorbed unwillingness to receive and respond to divine goodness the unwillingless that in life one was always cultivating God is being totally just and had done what is entirely right. Self hated and God hated will feed each other in Hell forever" (*Calvary Contender*, Dec. 15, 1991).

➢ **Church of England**:

"The Church of England has redefined Hell. Rather than a place of eternal suffering, Hell is a state of nothingness, the church said. The church said it was concerned that people were terrified into becoming believers and consequently suffered 'searing psychological scars." Nevertheless, everyone still faces a day of judgment, according to the Anglican document The Mystery of Salvation. Those who fail the test are annihilated. Hell is described as the final 'choosing of that which is opposed to God so completely and so absolutely that the only end is non being' (*National & International Religion Report*, Jan. I22, 1996).

➢ **Bill Phipps** (Moderator, United Church of Canada):

"I have no idea if there is a Hell. I don't think Jesus was that concerned about Hell. He was concerned about life here on earth...is Heaven a place? I have no idea" (*Ottawa Citizen*, Oct. 23, 1997).

➢ **American Baptist Convention**: In a survey taken in 1987 by the American Baptist magazine, it was found that only 59.8% agreed that "Hell is just punishment for sinners." 17.1% disagreed and 23.1% were "not sure."

➢ **David Jenkins** (Retired Anglican bishop of Durham):

"I am clear that there can be no Hell for eternity our God could not be so cruel. However, I think for some people who have wasted every opportunity for redemption, there may be extinction" (*The Advertiser*, Australia, Dec. 15, 1993).

➢ **Martin Luther King, Jr**:

"I do not believe in Hell as a place of a literal burning fire" (*Ebony* magazine, January 1961).

➢ **C. S. Lewis**:

"British author C.S. Lewis said Hell is not a place God sends people who disbelieve the gospel but a state of mind one chooses to possess and become. 'And every state of mind, left to itself,' he wrote, **'every shutting up of the creature within the dungeon of its own mind is, in the end, Hell"** (Lewis, *The Great Divorce*, p. 65)" (Calvary Contender, June 15, 1991).

➢ George Ladd (Fuller Seminary):

"Hell will be an eternity outside of fellowship with God and the enjoyment of the blessing of God…"

➢ **Nels F. S. Ferre**:

"According to the very meaning of soverign love, however, God both can and will have all to be saved. The Bible, in its largest and deepest logic, also affirms that with God all things are possible and that He would have all to be saved and come to the knowledge of the truth. **Among the numberless unthinking people and immature and unworthy eschatology espousing eternal Hell is unfortunately still prevalent**, vitiating (*making imperfect; perverting*) Christian ethics at its very heart? (Nels F.S. Ferre, "*Present Responsibility and Future Hope, Theology Today*, Jan. 1952, p. 493).

➢ **George Buttrick** (President Federal Council of Churches):

"A God who punishes men with fire and brimstone through all Eternity would hardly be Godlike. He would be almost satanic in cruelty and childlike in imagination – like a nasty little boy pulling off the wings of a fly. The Christian faith is that God and hereafter is like Christ" (Buttrick, *The Christian Fact and Modern Doubt*, 1935, p. 283).

➢ **Gerald Kennedy** (Methodist Church USA):

"Speaking of eternal punishment of an everlasting state of agony for the wicked. I can say that I am sure that God is at least as good and merciful as men. I certainly would not banish any man to a place of punishment forever because of his faults or his state of mind when he left this life. I am sure God is not less fair or merciful than I' (NAE magazine, Aug. 15, 1951).

➢ **Ruth Carter Stapleton** (sister of ex-president Jimmy Carter):

"The Bible does not teach that we experience Hell after we die, we experience it before we die" (*Christianity Today,* November 4, 1977).

If the writer understands these poor demented souls and their gross Bible ignorance, he has to assume they have been reading "funny books" instead of the Bible. The Bible sheds a lot light upon these confused commentators. Apparently, it is cruel for God to punish deserving sinners, but it is alright for God to allow His Only Begotten Son to be trampled upon, falsely accused, beard plucked out, beaten mercilessly with a whip containing bone or metal fragments, spit upon, crucified, pierced in His side, and have His precious blood mocked by Hell deserving religious bigots...

God did not spare **Israel and the Gentiles**. Both are yet to endure the worst historical judgment of all time in the future Great Tribulation:

Romans 11:21:

"For if God spared not the natural branches (Israel)..."

God did not spare **the angels** that sinned:

2 Peter 2:4:

"For if God ***spared not the angels*** *that sinned, but cast them down to Hell..."*

God did not spare **the Old World** that sinned. **2 Peter 2:5:**

And ***spared not the old world****, but saved Noah the eighth person, a preacher of righteousness, bringing in the flood upon the world of the ungodly.*

Again, God did not even spare **His own Son**. **Romans 8:32:**

> *"He that **spared not** H**is own Son**, but delivered Him up for us all..."*

What is all this foolish tommy-rot of man being so wonderful that God would not punish him with literal fire and if so, not very long?

NOTE: The writer is not the least bit impressed with the theologies and philosophies of well-known national preachers.

CHAPTER 6
THE STING OF DEATH

> *"The sting of death is sin; and the strength of sin is the law"* (I Corinthians 15:56)

From this verse, we see that the venom called sin is the parent of death.

To the "true" believer in Christ Jesus, death is **I Corinthians 15: 55, 57**,

> *"O death, where is thy sting? O grave, where is thy victory? But thanks be to God, which giveth us the victory through our Lord Jesus Christ".*

H. G. Well's well-publicized book "1984," which was made into a movie, depicts a brainwashing techniques of subjecting an unwilling citizen to his worst fears in order to shock him into submission to "Big Brother's control. The fear of rats was the "king of terror" for the main character (I think that he had a close relative eaten of rats). What does the reader fear? What is the king of terror for the reader? Is it death; Hell; judgment; torment?

The king of terror is DEATH for the unsaved person:

The saved person may dread the pain leading up to death but not the death itself. The lost sinner is thoroughly terrorized by the thought of death (if he is not, he is a greater fool than this writer imagined). Of course, some foolish sinners may mock at death but when death calls on him, he is shocked into sanity. It has been stated by some that witnesses to the death of atheists have stated that they never wanted to see another atheist die. The screaming, thrashing of the body, and horror on their face is convincing.

> Hebrews 9:27: *"And as it is appointed unto man once to die, but after this the judgment."*

The writer witnessed an unusual death:

The writer has not forgotten a frightening scene that he witnessed in a hospital many years ago. As I walked down a hospital corridor one evening and approached the door of a certain hospital room, the door burst open and a lady ran down the hall screaming as if some hideous monster was pursuing her. My first thought was that someone in the room that she knew was dying and she was running for help. Because the door was flung wide open, I had a full view of what scared the lady so much. A man was dying in a horrible way. I watched as his body convulsed in powerful contortions and literally leaped upwards. As his body thrashed violently, it rose upwards to an unbelievable height from the bed towards the ceiling. The man's face (which was very pale and ghostly looking) appeared to be in a fixed-stare upon something very frightening even as the body thrashings and levitations continued. I had the immediate thought that the man was unsaved and had been given a glimpse into Hell itself or perhaps into the face of demons. Perhaps some wicked in dying have seen the horror of Hell just as clearly as some saved people upon dying have seen the bliss of Heaven. I supposed that he was glimpsing the horror of Hell and resisting death with all of his might to prevent entering. Let me die the death of the righteous.

> **Numbers 23:10:** *"Who can count the dust of Jacob, and the number of the fourth part of Israel? **Let me die the death of the righteous**, and let my last end be like his!"*

It would be hard to imagine that a child of God would resist death so violently and react in such a manner. Perhaps the reader is not impressed with this death account, but I am sure if the reader had actually witnessed the bizarre scene, he would have been moved one way or the other. The writer may be wrong in his assessment of this deathbed scene but Scriptures teach a literal Hell and judgment. What a horrible way to die!

Death is the king of terror for the lost man.

> **Hebrews 9:27:** *"And as it is appointed unto man once to die, but after this the judgment."*

Why is Sin the Sting of Death?

Death was the result and punishment of sin.

> Romans 5:12: *"Wherefore, as by one man sin entered into the world, and death by sin; and so death passed upon all men, for that all have sinned."*

Some people may reason, "Why should I have to pay for Adam's sin? Unsaved people are not condemned for Adam's sin. Although all are born sinners in the sense of inheriting Adam's fleshly nature (sinners by birth), the truth is that all people also practice sin or have sinned (I John 1:8, 10). We are double sinners, both by birth and practice. An innocent baby that dies at an early age is not charged with Adam's sin debt, being yet innocent. Sin is not charged (imputed) to the baby. The baby that dies in innocence will go to Heaven. Sin has not been charged to the account of the baby just because of its natural birth! God's grace takes care of it. King David knew that one day he would see his dead baby again. When a person matures to the point of being accountable for his sin (only God knows for certain), Christ's righteousness may be imputed to him when he is willing to repent and confess Christ as his Lord and Saviour. Christ takes our sin upon Himself and we take His righteousness. Our sin is imputed (charged) to Christ and His righteousness is imputed to us. Christ nailed our sins to the cross of Calvary - (**Colossians** 2:14; 1:20; **Hebrews** 12:2).

Can a Christian NOT Sin?

Can a Christian NOT sin? Answer: Yes. God has commanded us not to sin and He would not command us to do the impossible. For every temptation, there is a way to escape - (**I Corinthians 10:13**). In Christ, every provision necessary to not sin has been provided by God. We are without any legitimate excuse whenever we commit or practice sin. However, this cannot be misconstrued to mean that some Christians *never* sin! Temptation itself is not sin; it is the yielding to the temptation that becomes sin.

Actually, sin alone is not the final ruin of man, it is man's failure to repent. **Luke 13:3, 5:**

> ***3*** *"I tell you, Nay: but, except ye repent, ye shall all likewise perish.*
> ***4*** *Or those eighteen, upon whom the tower in Siloam fell, and slew them, think ye that they were sinners above all men that dwelt in Jerusalem?* ***5*** *I tell you, Nay: but, except ye repent, ye shall all likewise perish."*

For all have sinned - (Romans 3:23; I John 1:8, 10).

> **Romans 3:23** *"For all have sinned, and come short of the glory of God;"*

> **1 John 1:8** *"If we say that we have no sin, we deceive ourselves, and the truth is not in us."*

CHAPTER 7

WHY DOES DEATH HAVE SUCH A STRANGLEHOLD ON MAN?

Again, Death is the ultimate effect of sin.

Romans 6:23: *"For the wages of sin is death...."*

Romans 6:23 *"For the wages of sin is death; but the gift of God is eternal life through Jesus Christ our Lord."*

The Law could not conquer death (it condemned to death) nor could the Law abolish death. The Gospel brings life and immortality. **Romans 6:23:** *"...the gift of God is eternal life."*

The Sting Of Death Is Sin; The Wages Of Sin Is Death!

Usually, a person does not really face the gravity of sin until he believes he is about to die. For many, it is too late. The Spirit of God has to draw a man to salvation in the time of grace that God has allocated to man. A sinner cannot wickedly plot to "live it up" in the present and call upon God at the latter end, thinking to use God as a fire-escape from Hell. Think about this, "Why doesn't everybody call upon God for mercy and salvation when they know that they are dying?" Why aren't nearly all people saved? They would have everything to gain and nothing to lose. It has been suggested that the reason that many near-death people do not respond to any thing of a spiritual nature is because they are so "doped up" or drugged. We know that most people die unsaved because Jesus taught that most people die lost and only a few will believe. **Matthew 7:13-14:**

> *"Enter ye in at the strait gate: for wide is the gate, and broad is the way, that leadeth to destruction, and many there be which go in thereat: Because strait is the gate, and narrow is the way, which leadeth unto life, and few there be that find it."*

The Nearness of Death:

Has the reader ever had an experience when he or she thought that they might be dying? The writer thought so once. The writer was over exposed to the gaseous fumes of perchloroethylene dry cleaning fluid while servicing a dry cleaning machine. As I felt my strength rapidly leaving me, I quickly sat down upon the floor to keep from crashing into it. Thinking that I might be dying, I remember thinking how sudden and unexpectedly that death may come. I found myself very repentant toward God, wanting to confess my sins and failures in so many ways. I thought, "Death may come so soon and unexpected. Why didn't I stop to give more thought about eternal things when I had plenty of time?" All of these thoughts meshed together in such a short time!

The thing that makes death terrible is sin. What a sinner enjoys today will sting tomorrow. Sinners don't get rid of sin at the Great White Throne

Judgment Bar. However, the sin of saint's has been settled before we die – at the cross of Jesus Christ.

If a person dies in their sin (unsaved), they go to Hell and they get worse and worse. **Revelation 22:11:**

> *"He that is unjust, let him be unjust still: and he which is filthy, let him be filthy still: and he that is righteous, let him be righteous still: and he that is holy, let him be holy still."*

- Hell is forever, just as long as Heaven lasts.
- Death is the king of terror for the lost man.

Unbeliever's Voices Near Death:

- **Voltaire**. At the point of death, Voltaire (1778), the well-publicized atheist, cried out, "I'm abandoned by God and man!" Then he said to his doctor, "Dr. Trochin, I'll give you half of what I'm worth if you will give me six months more of life." The doctor replied, "That cannot be."

Voltaire answered, "Then I shall go to Hell, and you will go with me!" And in his dying breath, he exclaimed, "O Jesus Christ!" Then he died.

It is obvious that Voltaire was no longer an atheist. He believed that he was going to Hell, a place that he had not believed in before.

- Actor **Charles Churchill** died in 1764. As he died, he said, "What a fool I have been!"

IT STUNG. Why? Because of sin.

- **Edward Gibbon (1794)** – author of *History of the Decline and Fall of the Roman Empire*, just before he died, said, "All is now lost, finally, irrevocably lost. All is dark and doubtful. I know not where I'm going!"

IT STUNG. Hell will sting far worse.

- **Mazarin** (1661) a French cardinal and statesman: "Oh, my poor soul! What will become of thee? Whither will thou go?"

- As **Thomas Paine** died, he said, "O Lord, help me, for I cannot bear to be left alone! Please Lord, send even a child to play with me!"

IT STUNG. There is no help in Hell.

- **Thomas Hobbes** died in 1679. When dying, he said, "I'm about to make a leap into the dark!"

He had no place for his feet. IT STUNG. Hell is a place of darkness.

- **Charles IX** (1754) a king of France: "What blood, what murders, what evil counsels have I followed! I am lost! I see it well!"

- **Sir Thomas Scott** (1500) a chancellor of England: "Until this moment, I thought there was neither God nor Hell; now I know and feel that there are both, and I am doomed to perdition by the just judgment of the Almighty!"

There is sober truth when an unbeliever faces death.

The rich man died and went to Hell and said, "I am tormented in this flame. IT STUNG. The rich man did not go to Hell because he was rich. He went to

Hell because he neglected God's provision for salvation. Wealth is a great entrapment for the soul of man. Man relies upon his money to sustain him. For everyone that dies lost, IT WILL STING ETERNALLY.

Death is the king of terror for the lost man.

Can a Man Know the Day of his Death?

There were people in the Bible that knew the approximate season of their death:

➢ **Moses** lost his temper and spoke unadvisedly and was told by God to prepare for death.

➢ **Aaron** displeased the Lord and met an early death.

➢ **Hezekiah** was given 15 years more on his life but he probably did not know the exact day.

➢ In **Noah's Flood**, obviously, all but Noah and his family knew that they would soon drown. Probably many attempted to cling to Noah's ark.

➢ The apostle **Paul** knew that his time to be beheaded was at hand (and many other martyrs).

Though some may know when their life is about to be extinguished, most do not know. However, God knows when our candle of life will be put out (**Job** 18:5, 6; 21:17; **Proverbs** 24:20).

> **Job 18:5** *"Yea, the light of the wicked shall be put out, and the spark of his fire shall not shine.* **6** *The light shall be dark in his tabernacle, and his candle shall be put out with him."*

> **Job 21:17** *"How oft is the candle of the wicked put out! and* how oft *cometh their destruction upon them!* God *distributeth sorrows in his anger."*

> **Proverbs 24:20** *"For there shall be no reward to the evil man; the candle of the wicked shall be put out."*

It is not so important "when we die" but "how we die." Certainly, the martyrs knew this better than most. **Ecclesiastes 9:12:**

> *"For man also knoweth not his time: as the fishes that are taken in an evil net, and as the birds that are caught in the snare; so are the sons of men snared in an evil time, when it falleth suddenly upon them."*

The medical doctors had thought the writer's aunt had little time to live (cancer) but she lived 50 years longer. A local young pharmacist (Greenville, SC) went for a full physical examination and was pronounced in perfect health by his doctor. He died the same week of a heart attack.

> **Ecclesiastes 8:8:** *"There is no man that hath power over the spirit to retain the spirit; neither hath he*

power in the day of death: and there is no discharge in that war; neither shall wickedness deliver those that are given to it."

No one reading this (saved or lost) has the guarantee that they will awaken tomorrow morning? A well-known evangelist frequently stated, "You are only one heartbeat from eternity." The Bible certainly supports this statement. Even if we live a full number of years, our life is as a *"vapor, that appeareth for a little time and vanisheth away."* (**James** 4:14).

The bravest, dullest, and most foolish man of all others is one that neglects his eternal life in favor of pleasing his contemporary life (the atheist does not count here for he is plain stupid).

Psalms 14:1: *"The fool hath said in his heart, There is no God..."*

Probably this fool is not necessarily in reference to an atheist nor a mentally retarded person but to a foolish, self-reliant man that says there is no God "for me." Read Romans, chapter 2, and note this, ***Psalms 19:1 says:***

The heavens declare the glory of God; and the firmament showeth His handiwork

Should a pagan desire salvation, the Gospel is displayed in the stars and the luminaries shine as to broadcast the glory of God and hope for the sinner. If a heathen person is willing to receive truth, God will send him/her a missionary or by means of the Word of God to save him.

CHAPTER 8

CAN A PERSON BE ASSURED OF HEAVEN WHEN HE DIES?

Answer: Yes, if that person is willing to accept God's Word as the final answer. The writer of the book of Hebrews admonishes believers to be diligent of their labor and cling to **the hope** (not cling to salvation itself) of their salvation to the end.

> **Hebrews 6:11:** *"And we desire that every one of you do shew the same diligence to the* ***full assurance*** *of hope unto the end."*

> ***Ecclesiastes 3:14:*** *"I know that,* ***whatsoever God doeth, it shall be for ever****: nothing can be put to it, nor any thing taken from it: and God doeth it, that men should fear before him."*

> *Philippians 1:6: "Being confident of this very thing, that he which hath begun a good work in you will perform it until the day of Jesus Christ."*

Of course, that "good work" wrought by God is salvation.

Many foolishly reason that they can go to Heaven because-they are doing the best they can or, they are keeping the 10 Commandments or, they have been baptized or, their **good works will be counted** or, they are trusting their church ordinances ("so-called" sacraments).

In the last two weeks, this writer was told by two different persons that they believed that they would go to Heaven if their good works outweighed their bad works. Then I quoted them Scriptures that discounted good works for salvation (Ephesians, 2:8-9; Titus 3:5; Galatians 2:16).

> **Ephesians 2:8** *"For by grace are ye saved through faith; and that not of yourselves: it is the gift of God: **9** Not of works, lest any man should boast."*

> **Titus 3:5** *"Not by works of righteousness which we have done, but according to his mercy he saved us, by the washing of regeneration, and renewing of the Holy Ghost;"*

> ***Galatians 2:16*** *"Knowing that a man is not justified by the works of the law, but by the faith of Jesus Christ, even we have believed in Jesus Christ, that we might be justified by the faith of Christ, and*

not by the works of the law: for by the works of the law shall no flesh be justified."

They did not appear to even listen (actually, the writer knew that these two persons had little or no good works whereof to mention. Regardless, God's Word will not return unto Him void – Isaiah 55:11).

Isaiah 55:11 *"So shall my word be that goeth forth out of my mouth: it shall not return unto me void, but it shall accomplish that which I please, and it shall prosper in the thing whereto I sent it."*

Some dare to say they are keeping the Law! But that is adding to sin. Keeping the Law gives strength to sin. How? No man can keep the Law! The Law says, **"Thou shalt not..."** The Law makes great demands and that is why sin is so strong. The strength of sin is the Law. If we could keep all the Law (and we cannot) and yet offend in one point, we are guilty of breaking all of the Law.

James 2:10: *"For whosoever shall keep the whole law, and yet offend in one point, he is guilty of all."*

When this writer and his preachers-friends were ministering publicly (in the 1960's) in a neighborhood (with loudspeakers) one afternoon, a religious gentleman approached this writer and stated, "I do not sin." Now the gentleman may have meant that he did not enjoy nor commit obvious "so-called" major outward (overt) sins of the flesh, but he did not elaborate on it. (We are admonished to not sin (**John** 8:11; **Exodus** 20; **Ezekiel** 8:11) and would not have been commanded so if it were not possible to "not sin.") The neighborhood man walked off silently after I had pointed him to **I John** 1:8, 10 and **Romans** 3:10-12, 23.

> I John 1:8: *"If we say that we have no sin, we deceive ourselves, and the truth is not in us."*

> *Ezekiel 18:4: "The soul that sinneth, it shall die."*

It is appointed to men once to die and after that the judgment (**Hebrews 9:27**).

> **Hebrews 9:27** *"And as it is appointed unto men once to die, but after this the judgment:"*

In Ezeekiel 18:4 (see above), it appears that Ezekiel is referring to the Second Death, eternal death of Revelation 20:14). However, a saved person that refuses to stop sinning, may meet an early death, **I John 5:16; Romans 6:16**:

> ***1 John 5:16*** **"***If any man see his brother sin a sin which is not unto death, he shall ask, and he shall give him life for them that sin not unto death. There is a sin unto*

death: I do not say that he shall pray for it."

Romans 6:16 *"Know ye not, that to whom ye yield yourselves servants to obey, his servants ye are to whom ye obey; whether of sin unto death, or of obedience unto righteousness?"*

Saved as if By Fire

But he himself will be saved (**I Corinthians 5:5**) and may lose his rewards (**I Corinthians 3:13-15**).

1 Corinthians 5:5 *"To deliver such an one unto Satan for the destruction of the flesh, that the spirit may be saved in the day of the Lord Jesus."*

1 Corinthians 3:13" *Every man's work shall be made manifest: for the day shall declare it, because it shall be revealed by fire; and the fire shall try every man's work of what sort it is.* ***14*** *If any man's work abide which he hath built thereupon, he shall receive a reward.* ***15*** *If any man's work shall be burned, he shall suffer loss: but* *he himself shall be saved; yet so as by fire."*

The sins of the saved person were judged at Calvary by Jesus' propitiation by His shed blood. (The saved person will only be judged for his faithfulness, stewardship, and rewards, not sin.)

The Judgment Seat of Christ

NOTE: A saved person will face the Judgment Seat of Christ to be judged for his stewardship (works) and faithfulness. This judgment determines the gain or loss of any rewards that he might receive. However, he will not be judged for sins because Jesus took all the sins of the saved man upon Himself at the cross of Calvary. The saved man's sin (past, present, and future) was imputed to Christ and Christ's righteousness was imputed to the saved sinner. Some religions erroneously teach that only the past sins are forgiven for salvation. When Christ died for our sins, all of them were future sins. Of course, any present or future sin may mar the fellowship with Christ.

Death to the unsaved person is a terrible monster. **Death is the "king of terror" for the lost.** Death may also be the king of terror to some Christians who do not have full assurance of their salvation. **Death has an eternal sting for the lost**. For the saved man, it is "O death, where is thy sting? O grave (hades), where is thy victory?

Assurance of Salvation

The Bible is our authority. The Bible says we can **have assurance** of Heaven.

I John 5:11-13: *And this is the record, that God hath given to us eternal life, and this life is in his Son. He that hath the Son hath life; and he that hath not the Son of God hath not life. These things have I written unto you that believe on the name of the Son of God; that ye may know that ye have eternal life, and that ye may believe on the name of the Son of God.*

There is no greater assurance than the Word of God (greater than an angel from Heaven). It is the **only** authority concerning man's soul.

See **John** 10:27-28; **Romans** 8:35-39.

John 10:27 *"My sheep hear my voice, and I know them, and they follow me:* **28** *And I give unto them eternal life; and they shall never perish, neither shall any man pluck them out of my hand."*

Romans 8:35 *"Who shall separate us from the love of Christ?* shall *tribulation, or distress, or persecution, or famine, or nakedness, or peril, or sword?"*

CHAPTER 9

IS THERE A "SECOND CHANCE" AFTER DEATH?

As has already been stated in this writing, there is no second-chance for salvation in the next world to come. There are many lost people who are deceived into believing that they will be afforded a "second chance" for Heaven after death. They are taught that there is a purgatory (place of purging sin), limbo state, or middle-place where they will be able to absolve their sins and eventually enter into Heaven. Many others are relying upon soul-damning "doctrines of devils" such as re-incarnation or soul-transmigration. Either these persons are brainwashed by phony religion or they are gullible and plain ignorant. They certainly are callous.to allow themselves to be robbed of their souls with demonic doctrines. They cannot find such teachings in the Word of God. When deceived people (some, "willingly ignorant") hear the plain truth of Scriptures, many attack the messenger rather than receive the truth of the Bible. Of course, many times, the matter boils down to "church authority" versus "Bible authority." A second chance of salvation for the unsaved does not follow death but judgment does.

> **Hebrews 9:27:** *"And as it is appointed unto men once to die, but after this the judgment."*

Neither is anyone going to be reincarnated into another life form (person, dog, cat, cow, rat, ape, skunk, amino acid, germ, or evolutionist/college professor), or given a second chance and eventually be purged of sin after many so-called soul transmigrations into various entities. There was national attention given to the pagan lie of reincarnation

In the 1950s at Pueblo, Colorado. Bridey Murphy of Pueblo claimed that she had lived a previous life in England and reincarnated to her present life. It was bjg news in Colorado Springs, where I was living only a few miles away. Much controversy followed. For sure, people who do not want to acknowledge that they are Hell-deserving sinners will swallow the "dunghill-doctrine" of a second-chance and lose their own souls. They will endear false teachings or false prophets above **The Word of God (KJV)**. It cannot be said too many times, **"After death, there is no second chance for the lost person."** Again, neither is there any such thing as purgatory. This non-existent middle-ground (which has been around for a long time) is bolstered by one particular religion in order to extract money from their parishioners. By rewarding a priest with monetary gifts, the donors are promised a shorter stay for their departed loved ones in the pseudo-land ("purgatory") in answerer to the priest's prayers for the deceased. The priest pledges prayers in order to obtain a shorter stay in the fabricated purgatory for the deceased loved-one in proportion to the amount of money given to him.

> **2 Peter 2:1-2:** *"But there were* ***false prophets*** *also among the people, even as there shall be*

> ***false teachers*** *among you, who privily shall bring in* ***damnable heresies****, even denying the Lord that bought them, and bring upon themselves swift destruction. And man shall follow their pernicious ways; by reason of whom the way of truth shall be evil spoken of."*

There are many lying spirits (**I John 4:6**) in the world today and consequently we have many cults, occults, sects, denominations, and religions. The antichrist spirits are pervading all kinds of false religions causing them to deny that Christ is come in the flesh.

> **1 John 4:6** *"We are of God: he that knoweth God heareth us; he that is not of God heareth not us. Hereby know we the spirit of truth, and the spirit of error."*

> **John 4:1-3: "***Beloved, believe not every spirit, but try the spirits whether they are of God: because* ***many false prophets*** *are gone out into the world. Hereby know ye the Spirit of God: Every spirit that confesseth that Jesus Christ is come in the flesh is of God: And every spirit that confesseth not that Jesus Christ is come in the*

flesh is not of God: and this is that spirit of antichrist, whereof ye have heard that it should come; and even now already is it in the world."

Of course, false religions are basing salvation upon church authority, good works outweighing bad works, church ordinances (sacramental salvation), treating their fellow man right, paying their honest dues, and doing the best they can. The best that we can do falls far short in the eyes of God. There is nothing wrong with good humanitarian works toward our fellow man and it is commended of us, but good works will not provide salvation nor assist to attain it (**Romans** 11:6; **Galatians** 2:16; **Titus** 3:5)).

Isaiah 64:6: *"But we are all as an unclean thing, and all our righteousnesses are as filthy rags; and we all do fade as a leaf; and our iniquities, like the wind, have taken us away."*

Romans 3:10: *"As it is written, There is none righteous, no, not one."*

Will everyone experience physical death?

Hebrews 9:27: *"And as it is appointed unto men* ***once to die*** *but after this the judgment:"*

Three Kinds of Death

There are T**hree Kinds of Death** mentioned in Scriptures: 1. Spiritual Death, 2. Physical Death, and 3. the Second Death:

1.) **Spiritual Death** is separation of a soul from God because of sin - (**Isaiah 59:2**; **John 5:24; Colossians 2:13**). Spiritual death is a reality for both the unsaved living and the dead lost. The unsaved living are spoken of as dead - (**Ephesians 2:1; I Timothy 5:6; John 3:18, 36).**

2.) **Physical Death** is separation of the spirit and soul from the body - (**Genesis 35:18; Ecclesiastes 12:7; Matthew 2:15; II Corinthians 5:8; James 2:26**).

- Both saved and unsaved people experience physical death.
- Resurrection is the opposite of physical death. Resurrection is body and soul together.
- Physical death in biblical usage never means extinction or non-existence.

3.) **The Second Death** (or eternal death) is the final, eternal separation of the unsaved from God - (**II Thessalonians 1:9; Revelation 20:14; 21:8**).

It has been said many times by many people, "An unsaved person is born once and dies twice; a saved person is born twice and dies once."

Believers may have to die physically (if not translated), but they will not die eternally.

The editor of the *Seventh Trumpet* magazine often told the true story of a traveler who, wandering through an old country cemetery, came upon a grave that caught his attention. It was marked with a stone, and upon it were these lines of poetry:

Pause, stranger, as you pass me by;

As you are now, so once was I;

As I am now, you too shall be,

So prepare for death and follow me.

The stranger paused a moment. As he thought of eternity, the suffering of the lost, then of the home of the redeemed with Christ in Heaven, he could not leave the cemetery till he wrote the two last lines:

To follow you, I am not content,

Until I know which place you went.

CHAPTER 10

WHAT ABOUT SOUL-SLEEP?

While resurrection is of the body and the body is spoken of as *asleep*, the spirit and soul of man continues to have consciousness and keenness of mind (acumen) after death. Consider the following passage of Scripture.

> ***Luke 16:22-31:*** *"And it came to pass, that the beggar died, and was carried by the angels into Abraham's bosom: the rich man also died, and was buried; And* ***in Hell*** *he lift up his eyes, being in torments, and seeth Abraham afar off, and Lazarus in his bosom. And he cried and said, Father Abraham, have mercy on me, and send Lazarus, that he may dip the tip of his finger in water, and cool my tongue; for* ***I am tormented in this flame****. But Abraham said, Son, remember that thou in thy lifetime receivedst thy good things, and likewise Lazarus evil things: but now he is comforted, and thou* ***art tormented.*** *And beside all this, between us and you there is a great gulf fixed; so that they which would pass from hence to you*

cannot; neither can they pass to us, that would come from thence. Then he said, I pray thee therefore, father, that thou wouldest send him to my father's house: For I have five brethren, That he may testify unto them, lest they also come in this place of torment. Abraham saith unto him, They have Moses and the prophets (Scriptures), neither will they be persuaded, though one rose from the dead."

Hell, or Hades, in this passage appears to be equivalent to the Old Testament Sheol, the place of departed spirits between death and resurrection. Neither Sheol nor Hades *specifically* denotes Hell, the place of final judgment. Hell is the *Tophet* (Hebrew) of the OT and the *Gehenna* (Greek) of the NT. Both Abraham and the rich man (although in different places) appeared to be very alert and perceptive concerning their environment. Both were also aware of their own past life on earth.

The rich man lift up his eyes...saw Abraham afar off

- ...Cried...have mercy on me...send Lazarus to dip the tip of his finger in water
- ...Said, I am tormented in the flame
- Interceded (or pretended to) for his brethren
- Abraham told the rich man...

- About the **impassable** gulf between them
- Of the **unchangeable** state of his agony
- Of the **hopelessness** of anyone who is not persuaded by **Scriptures**
- That the live brethren would not be persuaded though one raised from the dead...

Some claim that this passage is a parable. This patronizes the skeptics and modernists that disclaim a punishment for the lost. The modernists and liberals reckon that a parable is only a *figure of speech* and not to be taken literally. Although parables use figurative language, they represent something real in life or nature. A parable illustrates a principle or a truth in story form.

Examples

- Parable of the trees choosing a king - **Judges 9**
- Parable of the poor man and his lamb - **2 Samuel 12**
- Parable of the unjust judge - **Luke 18:1-8**
- Parable of the Pharisee and the publican - **Luke 18:9-14**

Although Jesus used many parables (some with fable content) to teach spiritual truths, the writer does not believe that this account is one. This story uses **proper names** (*Lazarus and Abraham)* and mentions **literal proper places**, *Hell* and *Abraham's bosom* (Paradise). Even if this account was a parable (the writer does not believe that it is), a parabolic illustration is never more profound than the truth represented by it. Neither does a figure or type exceed its antitype in its depth (profundity).

> *"...And in Hell he lift up his eyes, being in torments..."*

It is "torments" plural. The lost person will have to endure various sufferings in all his faculties or senses (feeling, sight, memory, isolation, etc.) for as long as Heaven lasts (forever).

Death is the king of terror for the lost person.

Soul-sleep

What about "soul-sleep" between death and resurrection?

"Sleep," when used in reference to death, is an affectionate term describing **the state of the body** of the believer after death. Between death and resurrection, the soul and spirit of man departs from the body, leaving the natural body inactive or asleep. Simply speaking, this is physical death. Jesus spoke of death as sleep. Sleep is "body death" - (**John 11:11-14; Matthew 27:52; Acts 7:54-60; Acts 13:36; I Corinthians 15:20**).

> **John 11:11** *"These things said he: and after that he saith unto them, Our friend Lazarus sleepeth; but I go, that I may awake him out of sleep.* **12** *Then said his disciples, Lord, if he sleep, he shall do well.* **13** *Howbeit Jesus spake of his death: but they thought that he*

had spoken of taking of rest in sleep. ***14*** *Then said Jesus unto them plainly, Lazarus is dead."*

Matthew 27:52 *"And the graves were opened; and many bodies of the saints which slept arose,"*

The false doctrine of soul sleep came about by a misunderstanding of Jesus' Words - (**Matthew 9:24; Mark. 5:39; Luke 8:52; John 11:11-14**).

Matthew 9:24 *"He said unto them, Give place: for the maid is not dead, but sleepeth. And they laughed him to scorn."*

Luke 8:52 *"And all wept, and bewailed her: but he said, Weep not; she is not dead, but sleepeth."*

John 11:11-14: *"These things said He: and after that He saith unto them, Our friend* ***Lazarus sleepeth;*** *but I go, that I may awake him out of sleep. Then said His disciples, Lord, if he sleep, he shall do well. Howbeit Jesus spake of his death: but they thought that he had spoken of taking of rest in sleep. Then said*

> *Jesus unto them plainly, Lazarus is dead."*

Jesus was speaking of body-sleep, not soul-sleep. Jesus spoke of death as sleep because He has resurrection power. Even the souls under the altar in **Revelation 6** were not asleep.

> **Revelation 6:9-11:** *"And when he had opened the fifth seal, I saw under the altar the* ***souls*** *of them that were slain for the Word of God, and for the testimony which they held: And they cried with a loud voice, saying, How long, O Lord, holy and true, dost Thou not judge and avenge our blood on them that dwell on the earth? And white robes were given unto every one of them; and it was said unto them, that they should rest yet for a little season, until their fellow servants also and their brethren, that should be killed as they were, should be fulfilled."*

As the Scriptures reveal, there is no such thing as soul-sleep as some false religions teach. **Only the body sleeps...**until the resurrection.

- The martyrs of the Great Tribulation in Revelation chapter 6 were not yet in their glorified resurrection bodies. They were slain for their testimony of Jesus Christ and for His Word, yet they were very alert and cried with a loud voice.

- The rich man and Abraham were not asleep - (**Luke 16**).
- Moses and Elijah were not asleep when they were transfigured with Christ. (Matthew 17:2-3).

The expression "asleep in Jesus" or "asleep in Christ" (**I Corinthians 15:18**) refers to the believer only.

> **1 Corinthians 15:18** *"Then they also which are fallen asleep in Christ are perished."*

When the believer is absent from his body, he is present with the Lord – (**2 Corinthians 5:8**).

> **2 Corinthians 5:8** *"We are confident, I say, and willing rather to be absent from the body, and to be present with the Lord."*

However, in the Old Testament, the reference to "them that **sleep** in the dust of the earth" appears to be the bodies of both believers and unbelievers - (**Daniel 12:2**).

The Second Death

The second death is a state of conscious existence - (**Revelation 14:9-11; 20:10**). There is conscious existence for both saved and unsaved after death.

Someone has said, *The difference between death and sleep is in continuance. Sleep is a short death; Death is a long sleep*. Actually, soul-sleep is not taught in Scriptures so Death is a long nightmare of reality to the lost!

Death is the king of terror for the lost!

QUESTION: If the scene of the souls under the altar in Revelation 6 appears during the Great Tribulation, which follows after the resurrection (rapture), should they not have resurrection bodies already?

ANSWER: In the Bible, the resurrection is likened to a crop harvest of which there are three divisions (any farmer knows this). The three parts of the harvest are:

The Three Parts of the Harvest

1.) Firstfruits 2.) Harvest 3.) Gleanings

Study carefully the following text in the resurrection chapter of **I Corinthians**.

> ***1 Corinthians 15:20*** *But now is Christ risen from the dead,* and *become the firstfruits of them that slept.* ***21*** *For since by man* came *death, by man* came *also the resurrection of the dead.* ***22*** *For as in Adam all die, even so in Christ shall all be made alive.* ***23*** *But every man in his own order: Christ the firstfruits; afterward they that are Christ's at his coming.* ***24*** *Then* cometh *the end, when he shall*

> *have delivered up the kingdom to God, even the Father; when he shall have put down all rule and all authority and power."*

Notice that in the believer's resurrection (**I Corinthians 15:22-23**), every man is made alive **in his own order.** The writer believes that this **order** (Greek "tagma") concerns *time* (chronology), not *rank.*

Firstfruits

__1.) Firstfruits:__ The firstfruits of which *Christ had become the firstfruits of them that slept,* undoubtedly included the many bodies of the saints that were dead and came out of the graves after Christ's resurrection, and went into Jerusalem and appeared to many:

> ***Matthew 27:52*** *And the graves were opened; and many bodies of the saints which slept arose,* ***53*** *And came out of the graves after his resurrection, and went into the holy city, and appeared unto many.*

To the writer, this appears to be OT saints.

Also, the hundred and forty and four thousand sealed Jews (**Revelation 14:1-4**) are said to be firstfruits unto God and to the Lamb. Perhaps this means the first-fruits out of the Great Tribulation.

James 1:18 says that we should be *"a kind of firstfruits"* of His creatures, not the firstfruits.

Romans 8:23 says that we have the firstfruits **of the Spirit**.

(Firstfruit(s) = the first of any; earliest ripe of the crop; first-born among man and beast; firstfruits of the Jewish restoration or the firstfruits from the dead.)

Harvest

2.) Harvest: "...They that are Christ's at His coming" may be the main harvest of the first resurrection. See **I Corinthians 15:51-58** and **I Thessalonians 4:13-18**. The Church (Jew and Gentile) is included in this group.

However, others think these are those that come out of the Tribulation Period.

Gleanings

3.) Gleanings: Those Saints of "the end" appear to be the gleanings of the resurrection harvest that includes the tribulation Saints. See **Revelation 6:9-11; 7:14; 20:4-5**.

There are others that believe that these are those that were in natural mortal bodies that have not yet received resurrection bodies at the end of the Millennium.

The correct choice of the three parts of the resurrection may be militated by the following references:

- Notice that in the "first order" of the First Resurrection (**Matthew 27:52-53**), the term, "This is the first resurrection," **is not** used.

- Notice that in the "second order" of the First Resurrection (**I Thessalonians 4:16-17**), the term, "This is the first resurrection," **is not** used.
- However, in the "third order" of the First Resurrection (**Revelation 20:4-6**), the term, "This is the first resurrection," **is** used. This is when the saints of the Great Tribulation lived again.

This *third order* or the *gleanings* of the Great Tribulation completes the **Three Orders** of the First Resurrection Harvest of believers. These saints were beheaded for their witness of Jesus and for the Word of God. They had not worshipped the beast, neither his image, neither had received his mark.

Does Everyone that Believes in Heaven Also Believes in Hell?

As previously mentioned, in several religious polls (for whatever polls are worth), a much higher percentage of people reported to believe in a literal Heaven than in a literal Hell (about 20% in most polls). Again, the same authority (The Word of God) proclaims both to be literal places. You can't believe in one and not the other. Everything that God says about Hell is factual and literal.

Facts About Hell

- Hell was originally prepared for the devil and his angels (Matthew 25:41)
- Hell is a place for the devil's children (John 8:44)
- Hell is the abode of the damned
- Hell is a place of torments and flame (Luke 16:24)

- Hell is a place of wailing and gnashing of teeth (Matthew 13:42)
- Hell is a place of weeping (Matthew 8:12)
- Hell is a place of fire. (5 different times, the NT says the fires of God are forever.)
- Hell is a place of smoke (Revelation 9:2; 14:11)
- Hell is a bottomless pit (Revelation 9:1, 2, 11; 11:7; 17:8; 20:1, 3)
- Hell is a place of darkness forever (Matthew 8:12; 22:13; 25:30; 2 Peter 2:4, 17; Jude 6, 13)
- Hell is a place where the worm dieth not and the fire is not quenched (Mark 9:48)
- Hell is a place of no return (Luke 16:26)
- Hell is a place of everlasting destruction (2 Thessalonians 1:9)
- Hell is a place of everlasting punishment (Matthew 25:46)
- Hell is a place of everlasting burnings (Isaiah 33:14)
- Hell is a horrible tempest (Psalms 11:6)
- Hell is a place of sorrows (Psalms 18:5)
- Hell is a place of no rest (Luke 16:27)
- Hell is a lake of fire (Revelation 20:10, 14, 15; 21:8)
- Hell is a devouring fire (Isaiah 33:14)
- Hell is a furnace of fire (Matthew 13:42; Revelation 9:2)

- Hell is a place of torment with fire and brimstone (Revelation 14:10)
- Hell is a place of filthiness (Revelation 22:10, 11)
- Hell is the second death (Revelation 20:14)
- Hell is a place of no forgiveness (Matthew 12:32)
- Hell is never full (Proverbs 27:20)
- Hell is enlarged (Isaiah 5:14)

The King of Terror

Death is the king of terror for the lost person! Why?

- There is no second chance.
- There are torments
- It is everlasting punishment
- It is isolation from God and all else

The black American preacher of 'Olden-Times' said it right:

> "Eber-body talkin' 'bout Heb'n aint't going there!"

CHAPTER 11

WHERE IS HELL LOCATED AND WHO WILL BE THERE?

Where is Hell?

Hell appears to be in the opposite direction from Heaven. Hell is always "down."

The apostle of Paul was caught "up" into the third Heaven. Elijah went "up" in the fiery chariot. (This provokes a question! Was Paradise in a compartment of Hades in the earth's core, which is **down**?)

- The "lowest Hell" – (Deuteronomy 32:22)
- "...go down quick into Hell" – (Psalms 55:15)
- Hell is beneath - Isaiah 14:9
- Angels that left their first estate were cast down to Hell – (Jude 6)
- Jesus descended "into the lower parts of the earth." – (Ephesians 4: 8-10)
- "things under the earth" - Philippians 2
- 'bottomless pit" – (Revelation 9:1). To be bottomless, it has to be down.
- Hell is called an abyss or pit – (That has to be down.)
- The Korahites went down. The earth opened up and swallowed them <u>up</u> (or down) into sheol, alive into Hell – (Numbers 16:32, 33).

It is not good to be side-tracked on the "location" of Hell. The fact that the Bible declares Hell to be a literal place of torment is enough. **Hell "is."** It is the opinion of many Bible students that Hell is now in the center of this earth. See **Deuteronomy** 32:22; **Numbers** 16:33; **Proverbs** 15:24; **Isaiah** 14:9; **Amos** 9:2; **Matthew** 12:40.

Who Will Be in Hell?

> **Revelation 21:8:** *"But the fearful, and unbelieving, and the abominable, and murderers, and whoremongers, and sorcerers, and idolaters, and all liars, shall have their part in* ***the lake which burneth with fire and brimstone****: which is the second death."*

> **I Corinthians 6:9-10:** *"Know ye not that the unrighteous shall not inherit the kingdom of God? Neither fornicators, nor idolaters, nor adulterers, nor effeminate, nor abusers of themselves with mankind, Nor thieves, nor covetous, nor drunkards, nor revilers, nor extortioners, shall inherit the kingdom of God."*

We can call some by name that will be in Hell:

Cain, Ahab, Jezebel, Goliath, Antiochus Epiphanes, Nero, Pilate, Bloody Mary, Hitler, Stalin,

Eichmann, Ingersol, Voltaire, Antichrist, Satan (Lucifer), fallen angels, **all unbelievers**.

The "Road to Hell" is paved with good intentions such as, tomorrow, later, neglect, not now, and other lame reasons that will be the cause of the damnation of the soul. Heaven is for those willing to submit to Jesus "today." "Tomorrow," "later," and "why not" will be the most sorrowful words in an eternal Hell.

What About "Death-bed" Repentance?

The writer believes in "death-bed repentance," but it is exceptional in its occurrence. The thief on the cross with Jesus comes to mind; however, he did not plan it that way. Again, anyone thinking that they will use Jesus as a fire-escape in the final moments of their life will be greatly deceived. God graciously awards the day of grace in which a man can be saved. Each and every day is precious. While there is life, there is hope. A sinner cannot hope that ample future days will be allowed him to select his day of salvation. The present is all that is promised to the lost sinner.

> **2 Corinthians 6:2:** "*For he saith, I have heard thee in a time accepted, and in the day of salvation have I succoured the: behold,* ***now*** *is the day of salvation.*"

No man can come to Jesus except that he is drawn of God and salvation is only in Jesus Christ and His shed blood.

John 6:44: *"No man can come to me, except the Father which hath sent me draw him: and I will raise him up at the last day."*

What About "Death-bed" Rejection?

There is a time in life when a person can commit the unpardonable sin of rejecting Christ (known only by God). This unpardonable sin may be committed long before death.

Perhaps the unsaved person reading this believes that they are smarter than the following persons who **could not** be saved in the end of their life:

- **Thomas Paine** – "I would give worlds, if I had them, if the Age of Reason had never been published. O Lord, help me! "Christ, help me! Stay with me! It is Hell to be left alone."
- **Queen Elizabeth** – "All my possessions but for a moment of time!"
- **Napoleon Bonaparte** – "I died before my time, and my body will be given back to the earth to become food for worms. Such is the fate of him who has been called the great Napoleon. What an abyss lies between my deep miserly and the eternal kingdom of Christ!"
- **Talleyrand Perigord** – "I am suffering the pangs of the damned."
- **Jennie Gordon** – "The fiends, they come; O save me! They drag me down! Lost! Lost! Bind me, ye chains of darkness! Oh! that I might cease to be,

but still exist. The worm that never dies, the second death."

- **Caesar Borgia** – "I have provided, in the course of my life, for everything except death. Now, alas! I am to die, although entirely unprepared!"

CHAPTER 12

FOR WHAT PURPOSE WAS HELL CREATED & ENLARGES HERSELF?

Again, Hell was originally created for the devil and his fallen angels.

> **Matthew 25:41:** *"Then shall he say also unto them on the left hand, Depart from me, ye cursed, into **everlasting fire**, prepared for the devil and his angels."*

Heaven is a prepared place (John 14:1) for prepared people. Hell is a prepared place or a designated place for unprepared people. The unsaved will be intruders in Hell. No unbeliever can enter the kingdom of God except they repent and become as little children (**Matthew 18:3**).

How Has Hell Gotten Larger?

> **Isaiah 5:14:** *"Therefore Hell hath enlarged herself, and opened her mouth without measure: and their glory, and their multitude, and their pomp, and he that rejoiceth, shall descend into it."*

Hell was originally prepared for the devil and his angels but multitudes of people choose to go there. Not only fallen angels will be in Hell, but also much of earth's population of about 6,000 years will be in attendance. At the time of this writing, it is estimated that there are about six (6) billion people on earth.

Since the sinner rejects the sacrificial offering of God's Son on the cross of Calvary, he certainly cannot go to Heaven. There is no other place for him to go except Hell.

Anyone teaching or preaching any other Gospel (second chance after death; faith plus water baptism; faith plus good works; faith plus sacraments; faith plus priestly intercession; etc.) than Jesus Christ is cursed to Hell (**Galatians 1:8; Romans 11:6**).

> **Galatians 1:8** *"But though we, or an angel from heaven, preach any other gospel unto you than that which we have preached unto you, let him be accursed."*

> **Romans 11:6** *"And if by grace, then* is it *no more of works: otherwise grace is no more grace. But if* it be *of works, then is it no more grace: otherwise work is no more work."*

Hell is never full, and her mouth is always open, ready to receive her next deceived religious victim (the world masses are incurably religious). Of course, hordes of sincere but lost religious people will cling to their prophesying, casting out devils, and many wonderful works.

> **Matthew 7:22:** *"Many will say to me in that day, Lord, Lord, have we not* ***prophesied*** *in thy name? And in thy name have cast out devils? And in thy name done many wonderful works?"*

Jesus answers the false religionists:

> **Matthew 7:23:** *"And then will I profess unto them, I never knew you: depart from me, ye that work iniquity."*

CHAPTER 13

WHEN WAS HELL CREATED?

There is some debate about when God made Hell. If God had wanted us to know, He would have specifically told us when. The time of Hell's creation is not relevant to man's salvation. What is important and frightening is that Hell has its arms open to receive sinners. The only guarantee of a person's salvation is the present time, not tonight or tomorrow or sometimes later.

> **2 Corinthians 6:2:** *"...behold, **now** is the accepted time; behold, **now** is the day of salvation."*

> **Hebrews 2:3:** *"How shall we escape, if we **neglect** so great salvation..."*

If a person could select their "time" of salvation, probably many would elect to be saved at the end of their life. However, this contradicts the Words of Jesus. Jesus said that **many** would go in at the broad gate (destruction; Hell) and **few** would enter the strait gate (life; Heaven) - **Matthew 7:13-15.**

> **Matthew 7:13**: *"Enter ye in at the strait gate: for wide is the gate, and broad is the way, that leadeth to destruction, and many there be which go in thereat:* ***14*** *Because strait is the gate, and narrow is the*

> *way, which leadeth unto life, and few there be that find it.* **15** *Beware of false prophets, which come to you in sheep's clothing, but inwardly they are ravening wolves."*

How Does Unbelief Affect Faith?

The unbelief of some does not hinder the faithfulness and truth of God's Word.

> **Romans 3:3** *"For what if some did not believe? Shall their* ***unbelief*** *make the faith of God without effect? God forbid: yea, let God be true, but* ***every man a liar"***

The unbelief of those that reject Christ will not nullify the believer's salvation; neither will the unbeliever escape the judgment of God.

CHAPTER 14

DOES THE BIBLE TEACH "SOUL ANNIHILATION"?

False religionists teach that the unbeliever ceases to exist after death. The Hebrew word for soul "nephesh" can sometimes be translated "person," but isolated verses cannot be used to support an entire doctrine.

The unbeliever would gladly choose annihilation rather than everlasting punishment. The Bible does **not** teach soul annihilation but false religionists do. Annihilation instead of endless torment would be no punishment at all for the wicked dead. Fallen angels were not annihilated and still exist and their penalty is not extinction but suffering (Matthew 25:41). The soul does not cease to exist when the body dies. *Everlasting punishment* for the unsaved is taught in Scriptures as well as *everlasting life* for the saved. Of course, if a person's soul were annihilated in the lake of fire, then everlasting "annihilation" would apply, not everlasting "punishment." Everlasting punishment for the unsaved will last as long as everlasting life lasts for the believer. The Greek word "aionios" is translated both "eternal" and "everlasting:"

Aionion

- Aionios is translated as **eternal** in forty-two places of which thirty-nine refer to God, Heaven and spiritual life and joy; one judgment; two to future punishment –(Mark 3:29; Jude 7).

- Aionios is translated as **everlasting** in twenty-five places; twenty-one to God; four to future punishment (Matthew 18:8; 25:41, 46; 2 Thessalonians 1:9).

The saved enjoy eternal joy, but the unsaved suffer eternal ruin. The only interlude possible for the unsaved person is when death and Hell are delivered up for judgment at the **Great White Throne of God - (Revelation 20:11-15**).

> **Revelation 20:11** *"And I saw a great white throne, and him that sat on it, from whose face the earth and the heaven fled away; and there was found no place for them.*
> ***12** And I saw the dead, small and great, stand before God; and the books were opened: and another book was opened, which is the book of life: and the dead were judged out of those things which were written in the books, according to their works.*
> ***13** And the sea gave up the dead which were in it; and death and hell delivered up the dead which were in them: and they were judged every man according to their works.*
> ***14** And death and hell were cast into the lake of fire. This is the second death.*
> ***15** And whosoever was not found written in the book*

> *of life was cast into the lake of fire."*

Instead of "so-called" soul annihilation, the Scriptures teach that there is no rest for the wicked dead:

> **Revelation 14:11:** *"And **the smoke of their torment ascendeth up for ever and ever**: and they have no rest day nor night, who worship the beast and his image, and whosoever receiveth the mark of his name."*
>
> **Isaiah 33:14:** *"...Who among us shall dwell with the devouring fire? who among us shall dwell with **everlasting burnings**?"*
>
> **Matthew 18:8:** *"...it is better for thee to enter into life halt or maimed, rather than having two hands or two feet to be cast into (the) **everlasting fire**.*
>
> **Matthew 25:41:** *"Depart from me, ye cursed, into **everlasting fire** prepared for the devil and his angels."*
>
> **Matthew 25:46:** *"And these shall go away into **everlasting***

> ***punishment***: *but the righteous into life eternal."*

(***Everlasting and eternal*** = *"aionion."* Aionion is the adjective form of "aion."

Aion = "for the age," "unto the ages," " unto the ages of the ages," and

" everlasting without end." Aionion is the only way in Greek to say eternal or everlasting.

Aionion is used for...

1.) glory of God, **2.)** believers security, **3.)** punishment of the lost.)

> **Mark 9:43-48:** *"...to go into H**ell (Gehenna) into the fire that never shall be quenched**...Where their worm dieth not, and **the fire is not quenched**...to be cast into Hell (Gehenna) into **the fire that never shall be quenched**...Where their worm dieth not, and **the fire is not quenched**...Where their worm dieth not and **the fire is not quenched**."*

> **II Thessalonians 1:9:** *"Who shall be punished with **everlasting destruction** from the presence of the Lord, and from the glory of His power."*

Also see **Revelation 20:11-15; 21:8**.

The Eternal State

In eternity future, he that is righteous will be even righteous still (greater) but the unjust will never improve and it even appears that their condition will even worsen:

> **Revelation 22:11:** *"He that is unjust, let him be unjust still and he which is filthy, let him be filthy still: and he that is righteous, let him be righteous still: and he that is holy, let him be holy still."*

Actually, "endless misery" is not an alien concept to human reason and is the natural opposite of "endless happiness." A tree falls in the direction of inclination and remains there - (**Ecclesiastes 11:3**). Even the secular world has coined a good saying, "As the twig is bent, so is the tree inclined." The name of the wicked shall rot – (**Proverbs 10:7**).

In reference to sin and damnation, someone has said, "We sow a sin and reap a habit; we sow a habit and reap a character; we sow a character and reap a destiny. This is taught in Scripture – (*Galatians 6:7*). Character is like a stream of water that cuts its course deeper and deeper until the channel becomes fixed and permanent. Down in the gorge or pit of the second death, no echo of hope will ever be heard..."If only I had...too late...too late."

Future punishment in Hell is not corrective or remedial and is without remedy:

> **Proverbs 29:1:** *"He, that being often reproved hardeneth his neck, shall suddenly be destroyed, and that without remedy."*

Christ is the Judge and final court. There is no appeal. For the unsaved, **death is the king of terror** for afterward there is no "second chance."

What is the Worm in Mark 9:44, 47?

> **Mark 9:44, 47***: "Where their* ***worm*** *dieth not, and the* *<u>fire</u>* *is not quenched"* **Mark 9:47** *And if thine eye offend thee, pluck it out: it is better for thee to enter into the kingdom of God with one eye, than having two eyes to be cast into hell fire:*

The worm appears to be a metaphorical term describing man's low and feeble state. Their worm is taken from *Isaiah 66:24* where the people of God are looking upon the carcasses of men who had transgressed against God...the heaps of dead slain in battle and worms feeding on the dead. The worm shall not die as long as there are carcasses to be devoured and the bodies of the dead shall *continue long* to burn. This is a figure denoting great misery and terrible destruction. Hell is depicted as a state of decay, which is never completed, and burning which does not consume. The picture is one of worms or maggots feeding upon decaying dead bodies; hence, a description of the horrible torment and excruciating pain of **a lost person in Hell**. The ever-burning trash pile, in the valley of Hinnom on the south side of Jerusalem, was also a dumping place for unwanted dead bodies (animals, criminals, etc.) that were eaten by maggots and burned with fire. This high place in the valley of Hinnom was called *Tophet* (Gehenna/Hell in the N.T.).

The NT word *Ge-henna* is derived from the OT term *Ge-Hinnom*, valley of Hinnom, (valley of the sons of Hinnom).

In the OT, heathen parents made their children pass through fire to Moloch in this place that later came to be called Gehenna - (**2 Kings 16:3**; **17:17; 21:6; 23:10; 2 Chronicles 33:6; Isaiah 30:33; Jeremiah 32:35; Ezekiel 16:21; 20:31; 23:37**).

Even memory will be a perpetual torment in Hades, "...Son, remember" - **Luke 16:25**.

As it has been stated already, there would be no need for *everlasting fire* (**Matthew 25:41**) if souls were consumed or annihilated. If the soul ceased to exist, what purpose would be served by the burning of an eternal fire? There would be no reason for it's burning!

Death is the king of terror for the lost person.

Are there unusual types of earthly fire?

There are several unusual earthly fires mentioned in the Bible:

- There is the earthly fire which alludes to and is a type of Hell (Gehenna) fire. Jesus referred to Gehenna eleven times. The trash pile outside of Jerusalem was a type of the eternal Lake of Fire (the antitype) where "the fire that never shall be quenched" - **Mark 9:43-48**.

- A burning bush that was not consumed that Moses observed - See **Exodus 3:2**.
- The furnace heated seven times hotter that did not harm Shadrach, Meshach, and

Shadrach, Meshach, Abed-Nego (Daniel 3:19-26).

(Undoubtedly, the 4th man in the fire in this passages was Jesus in pre-incarnate form.

- Then the LORD rained upon Sodom and upon Gomorrah brimstone and **fire** from the LORD out of Heaven - (**Genesis 19:24**).

*P*erhaps this was lightning, but it was also specially ordered from the LORD.

- Then the **fire** of the LORD fell and consumed the burnt-sacrifice and the wood, and the stones, and the dust, and licked up the water that was in the trench - **I Kings 18:38**.

This special fire from God signified divine approval of an offering or sacrifice.

The words of Jesus are "final." Jesus did not warn with empty words just in order to frighten people into Heaven:

> **Mark 9:43-44:** *"And If thy hand offend thee, cut if off. it is better for thee to enter into life maimed, than having two hand to go into H***ell***,*

> *into the fire that never shall be quenched: Where their worm dieth not, and the fire is not quenched."*
>
> **Mark 9:45-46:** *"And if thy foot offend thee, cut it off: it is better for thee to enter halt into life, than having two feet to be cast into H**ell**, into the fire that never shall be quenched: Where their worm dieth not, and the fire is not quenched."*
>
> ***Mark 9:47-48:*** *"And if thine eye offend thee, pluck it out: it is better for thee to enter into the kingdom of God with one eye, than having two eyes to be cast into H**ell fire**: Where their worm dieth not, and the fire is not quenched"*

The warning of Hell by Jesus' own lips should be more than a catalyst to move a sinner to repentance.

Perhaps the three ways listed in Mark's Gospel (hand, foot, eye) correlate somewhat to three main avenues to sin and damnation listed in **I John 2:16:**

> *"For all that is in the world, the **lust of the flesh**, and the **lust of the eyes**, and the **pride of life**, is not of the Father, but is of the*

> *world. And the world passeth away, and the lust thereof: but he that doeth the will of God abideth for ever."*

"What is the Will of the Father?

> *"Jesus answered and said unto them, This is the work of God, that ye believe on Him whom He hath sent"* **John 6:29**.

Spiritual Gifts:

Speaking concerning spiritual gifts, Paul says in **I Corinthians 14:38**, "But if any man be ignorant, **let him be ignorant**."

If we make an application of gifts, the greatest gift ever given to man was not a talent in which we could boast of, such as the exercise of some spiritual gift imparted by the Holy Spirit (preach, teach, discern the spirits, speak in tongues, etc.), but the greatest gift of God to man was His Son for salvation.

> **Romans 6:23:** *"For the wages of sin is death; but the* ***gift*** *of God is eternal life through Jesus Christ our Lord."*

> **Ephesians 2:8-9:** *"For by grace are ye saved through faith; and that not of yourselves: it is the* ***gift***

of God: Not of works, lest any man should boast."

2 Corinthians 9:15: *"Thanks be unto God for His unspeakable **gift**."*

Romans 10:13: *"For whosoever shall call upon the name of the Lord shall be saved."*

The greatest gift a believer can give to an unbeliever is the Gospel of Jesus Christ, not a show of our spirituality. We are admonished, even commanded, to be witnesses of His saving grace.

How Well Believers Die!

- **John Wesley** (the great Methodist preacher) – Just before he died, he said, "Best of all, God is with us"
- **Billy Bray** (the famous Cornish miner) – The doctor came into his room and said, "Brother Billy, you're going to die."

Billy asked, "You mean soon!"

"Yes soon."

"Today?"

"Billy, today."

"Am I dying now?"

"Yes Billy, you're dying now."

"Glory! Glory! Glory to God! I'll soon be in Heaven."

- **A. J. Gordon** – When he died, he shouted "Victory."
- **D. L. Moody** (1I899) – "Earth recedes; Heaven opens before me. No, this is no dream, Well. It is beautiful. It is like a trance. If this is death, it is sweet. There is no valley here. God is calling me, and I must go. This is my triumph! This is my coronation day!"
- **John Antler** – "The chariot has come, and I am ready to step in."
- **Margaret Prior** (1842) – "Eternity rolls before me like a sea of glory!"
- **Martha McCrackin** – "How bright the room! How full of angels!"
- **Sir David Brewster** (1868) – inventor of the kaleidoscope: "I will see Jesus: I shall see Him as He is. I have had the light for many years. Oh, how bright it is! I feel so safe and satisfied!"

The **apostle Paul** was a champion Christian just as were many other martyrs (Stephen; Antipas; Peter, James, and seven other apostles (See *Foxes Book of Martyrs*). Paul did not whimper because he knew that to be absent from the body is to be present with the Lord. Paul said, *"I am now ready to be offered, and the time of my departure is at hand."*

> **Revelation 20:14-15**: *"And death and hell were cast into the lake of fire. This is the second death. And whosoever was not found written*

in the book of life was cast into the lake of fire."

John 5:40: *"And ye will not come to me, that ye might have life."*

It is not that a sinner "cannot" come to Christ for life, it is that he "will not" come.

For the lost person, the king of terror is death.

When speaking of the princes of the nations and especially of Pharaoh and Egypt, the Lord says,

*"...all of them...which are gone down with the slain...that go down to the pit...For I have caused, my terror in the land of the living..." (**Ezekiel** 32:30, 32).*

CHAPTER 15

NO PLACE TO ESCAPE THE JUDGMENT OF GOD

Though speaking of Israel in the book of Amos, the application can be made individually to any unbeliever:

> **Amos 9:2:** *"Though they dig into H**ell**, thence shall mine hand take them; thought they climb up to Heaven, thence will I bring them down."*

Neither is there any escaping the Spirit of God for the believer:

> **Psalm 139:7-8:** "*Whither shall I go from Thy spirit? Or whither shall I flee from Thy presence? If I ascend up into heaven, Thou art there: if I make my bed in Hell, behold, Thou art there."*

Jonah was a good example of a believer trying to escape God's will and was even brought down to the belly of Hell – (Jonah 2:2-3).

The writer believes that the principal reason that atheists and evolutionists desire to be cremated is because of the fear of God's judgment.

Of course, if God originally formed the atoms that man is made of (and He did), He certainly can reassemble them even though the bodies be decayed, eaten of animals, or **cremated**.

An infidel said, "There is one thing that mars all the pleasures of my life."

"Indeed!" replied his friend. "What is that?"

He answered, "I am afraid the Bible is true. If I could know for certain that death is an eternal sleep, I should be happy; my joy would be complete! But here is the thorn that stings me. This is the word that pierces my very soul—if the Bible is true, I am lost forever!"

The story is told of an atheist who delighted in mocking a young Christian about his belief concerning punishment in Hell for the lost. Though the lad was uneducated and slow of wit, he had the faith of a determined believer. He proposed a scenario to the atheist that most of us have already heard before, but is worth repeating: He told the atheist, "If my belief in Christ and the Bible is wrong and I die, I have lost nothing and neither have you. If my belief in Jesus Christ and the Bible is right and I die, I have avoided Hell for eternity and gained Heaven forever; but you have lost everything."

God is not willing than any should perish (2 Peter 3:9), but the devil walketh about seeking whom he may devour (I Peter 5:8). Someone has said, "God has cast a vote for you and the devil has cast a vote against you; only you can break the tie-vote."

In Hell, there will be:

- No evangelist or preacher

- No hell-fire and brimstone preaching
- No more pardon (no second chance)
- No water
- No rest (everlasting punishment)

God often delays the punishment of sin for a while, but it is laid up in store till the measure be full and the day of divine patience is over.

> **Job 21:28:30:** *"For ye say, Where is the house of the prince? And where are the dwelling places of the wicked? Have ye not asked them that go by the way? And do ye not know their tokens, That the wicked is reserved to the day of destruction? They shall be brought forth to the day of wrath."*

Hell

> *The damnation of Hell is the fire of God's anger fastening upon a sinner. Their foot shall slide in due time* – (Deuteronomy 32:35).

Death and Hell are the king of terror for the sinner!

NOTE: The writer is aware of the false claim by the Jehovah Witness cult that the grave is Hell. This claim is mainly based upon the fact that Greek "hades" is translated as "grave' in I Corinthians 15:55 of the KJV. However, Hades (OT "Sheol) was comprised of both Paradise and Hell. Consequently, Hades was the place of all of the dead, both saved and lost, not just those in Hell.

Heaven or Hell? Only the sinner himself can choose to repent of their sin and believe the Gospel that Jesus died as their sin sacrifice on Calvary...or neglect until it is too late.

God often delays the punishment of sin for a while, but it is laid up in store till the measure be full and the day of divine patience is over. For the believer, the remembrance of sin may add terror to death but a glimpse of Heaven will remove the fright.

Death is the king of terror to the unsaved. This writer believes the Bible (KJV).

ABOUT THE AUTHOR

The writer was born in Greenville, SC in 1934 and was a lifetime resident except for two years in the US Army (Fort Jackson, S.C. and Fort Carson, Colorado) and two years residence in Florida.

After separation (honorably) from the US Army, the writer returned to Greenville, SC and married at age 27 to Christine Moore, an old acquaintance from an adjacent neighborhood. The Lord blessed us with six daughters, Debbie, Donna, Dale, Denise, Deree, and Dena.

A short time after marriage, the writer was convicted of his lost condition as a sinner and after a miserable time under conviction the writer confessed his sin and lost condition to God and was saved.

The writer was 40 years of age when he began attending college (3 years, no diploma).

The writer retired as a chemical technologist from Morton International Chemical Company in 1996. Before retirement, the writer had the urge to write on Bible subjects and wished that he had more time to study. Upon retirement, the writer bought a computer and became a novice writer.

The writer now resides in Easley, S.C.

D. Helton has written several documents and books, as well as the books or booklets: "Jesus is God," "Evolution, Another False Religion of Humanism," "Cremation: Christian or Pagan," "Is The Gap Theory Credible?" "Does Water Baptism Save," "Can a Saved

Person Become Unsaved," and several others, available here:

http://www.theoldpathspublications.com/Pages/Authors/Helton.htm#God

Dennis Helton
200 Home Place Drive
Easley, SC 29640

www.ingramcontent.com/pod-product-compliance
Ingram Content Group UK Ltd.
Pitfield, Milton Keynes, MK11 3LW, UK
UKHW021921190726
13853UKWH00002B/784